Spokane and Coeur d'Alene

Freshwater

Shark Attacks

Spokane and Coeur d'Alene

Freshwater

Shark Attacks

James P. Johnson

Layout by Nancy Correll
Photographs by James P. Johnson
Printed by Gray Dog Press, Spokane, WA, USA
Contact author at Freshwatersharkattacks@gmail.com

Copyright 2022 by James P, Johnson

ISBN 979-8-9856226-0-7

The unauthorized distribution of this copyrighted work is illegal. Reproduction or transmission by any means without permission from the author except for brief passages in reviews or limited, non-commercial uses is prohibited.

High Fives to…

my sister, Nancy Correll. She did the layout, most of the front cover artwork and pointed out changes for me to consider along the way. A former technical writer at a large pharmaceutical firm, I picked up some fine points of grammar from her despite my 30 years of freelance writing experience. She put in a lot of hours after saying it sounded fun when I described the project and asked if she'd help.

a former newspaperman, Mike Schmeltzer, who has a career of experience in journalism. As a COVID precaution at a coffee shop, we sat at an outside table on a cold December day for over an hour while my hands reached absolute zero. I used his advice to make plenty of changes to my manuscript, and I value he took the time to read it and provide input. Declining a handshake as we parted and giving a fist bump instead surely spared him severe injury.

outdoor adventurer, Kirsten Frost Andersen, who volunteered to do some digital imaging work. Only one photo in the entire book is manipulated, but it's an important one.

a deputy director at a federal agency in Washington, DC, Tricia Van Orden, for approving my book. I did not need federal approval, but my daughter offered her opinion when I asked from time to time. She also read several of my landmark descriptions and reacted in a way that showed I was on the right path.

Caution Advisory

It's possible after reading a few pages of this book you'll experience intense agitation that could ruin your day beyond repair. You could become so annoyed and disgruntled, you'll find yourself shouting the below phrases or ones similar to them.

"You gotta be kidding!"   *"No Way!"*   *"This is so wrong!"*

What could follow next is this book flying across the room and slamming into the wall, unless you're aware this book is a parody.

Maybe the title piqued your curiosity. Do freshwater sharks really live around here? They've attacked people? When you read about the natural history of Lake Coeur d'Alene, you'll learn it originated as a bay on the Pacific Ocean and still contains a remnant population of great white sharks that attack swimmers every summer. You'll also find out in the first story (Riverfront Park) that sharks got into a waterslide complex there in the 1990s and made lunch out of so many swimmers.

However, following each spoofy account of the 37 Spokane and Coeur d'Alene landmarks that comprise this book, a one-word heading (Actually) directs you to an alternative account which may contain real facts.

But it's still your choice which one to believe. You get to decide whether the twin, brick, cylindrical towers in downtown Spokane were launch silos for NASA space missions in the 1960s, or part of a plant that produced steam heat for downtown buildings.

You choose whether The Carousel in downtown Spokane was created by the two-man team of Michelangelo and Leonardo da Vinci, eventually acquired by France and shipped to the United States with the Statue of Liberty as a bonus gift, or was made for a Spokane amusement park that operated from 1909 to 1968.

So, as you work your way through this book, accepting the version that works for you is fine. But it would please me if I overheard you telling your out-of-town relatives that Tubbs Hill was originally a mountain, became a lake, then a swamp and a meadow before finally becoming a hill because I'd know exactly where you got that.

Contents

Spokane

Riverfront Park	8
The Pavilion	10
The Carousel	12
Great Northern Clock Tower	15
Garbage Goat	16
Joy of Running Together Sculptures	18
Brick Deposits	20
Monroe Street Bridge	22
Spokesman-Review Tower	24
Fox Theater	26
The Steam Plant	28
Davenport Hotel	30
Spokane Intermodal Center	32
Duncan Gardens	34
Gonzaga University	36
Veterans Arena	38
Spokane County Courthouse	40
Centennial Trail	42
1000 Steps	44
Drumheller Springs	46
Mount Saint Michael	48
Comet Crater	50
Plante's Ferry	52
Grounded Submarine	54
Spokane House	56
Little Spokane River Natural Area	58
Vista House at Mount Spokane	60

Coeur d'Alene

Lake Coeur d'Alene	62
The Beach at Lake Coeur d'Alene	64

Coeur d'Alene Carousel	66
Coeur d'Alene Resort	68
Coeur d'Alene Floating Green	70
Fort Sherman	72
Fort Sherman Chapel	74
McEuen Park	76
Tubbs Hill	78
Mineral Ridge	80
End Notes	82

Riverfront Park

One of the youngest parks in the city, Riverfront Park was created following the World's Exposition of 1974. That's just 5 years old in park years!

Riverfront Park almost didn't come to be. The expo master plan dictated the grounds be returned to its original state—a network of decrepit trestles and abandoned buildings. However, Stephanie Moran, a Spokane high school student, advocated for a gravel pit because the plentiful basalt would generate income for the city. Her idea was nixed, but it opened the door for other ideas, and eventually a park was suggested.

The new park was built with several dazzling attractions. However, over the years, safety lapses caused numerous fatalities. The very popular Tarzan Swing across the Spokane River was shut down after only 5 months. A pair of auto mechanics on an after-work outing left oil and grease on the rope. The next 3 riders slipped into the river and drowned before a park employee noticed the problem.

In the late 1990s, a nighttime water fluctuation in a habitat featuring freshwater sharks native to the Spokane River washed a couple of them out of a pool, across a walkway, and into the adjacent Riverfront Waterslide Complex. The problem went unnoticed until the next day when lifeguards, thinking patrons were being especially rambunctious, became alarmed when everything turned calm, quiet and the water, dark red.

Despite safety issues of the past, the demand for edgy, thrill-seeking attractions continues. Enthusiasm is especially high for the new centerpiece of the park—The River Rapids Stand-up Paddleboard Race Course.

Actually…

There have been many attractions at Riverfront Park, but a Tarzan Swing across the river and a habitat featuring sharks indigenous to the Spokane River system were never among them. There are a few places in the world where sharks live in freshwater, but the Inland Northwest is not one of them.

Many features of the World's Fair were incorporated into the fabulous new park which officially opened in 1978, but the biggest was the creation of 100 acres of open space at the center of the city, situated at a major drop in the Spokane River that highlighted a beautiful landmark Spokane always had, but previously was hard to see and access. After decades of use, Spokane voters approved a $63.4 million bond in 2014 to update and renovate the park. The multi-year project was completed in 2021.

There are several features of the park that are well-known landmarks. However, the falls and rapids of the Spokane River are its centerpiece. Spokane is the rare city that has a significant river elevation drop at its downtown core. When the river is swollen during spring run-off, few urban waterways in the country can match the roar and thunder of Spokane's falls and rapids.

The Pavilion

What is now The Pavilion in Riverfront Park was originally built around 1450 by the Spokane Tribe of Indians. It was constructed for a contest among area tribes over who could build the biggest teepee. The Spokane Tribe won, and it still holds the world record for largest teepee ever built. Originally constructed of wood, braided bark and vines, and covered with a layer of dried animal skins, it was a meeting place for large gatherings.

With the coming of settlers and displacement of the Spokane Tribe, the teepee was taken over by Whites. It was used for festivals, large gatherings and many other events.

When Spokane was awarded the World's Fair of 1974, the teepee was repurposed for the U.S. Pavilion and was the largest exhibit of Expo '74. After Expo, the teepee was incorporated into Riverfront Park and in 2019, it was refurbished for the first time, more than 550 years after it was built.

Actually…

The Pavilion in Riverfront Park was originally the U.S. Pavilion for the World's Fair of 1974. Its main function was showing an IMAX movie about the environment on a huge screen. After Expo '74, the federal government gave the building to the city. It retained the IMAX theater, and over the years, contained an educational science center, ice rink, miniature golf course and amusement park rides for children.

The steel cable lattice supported a white vinyl covering, which degraded quickly after the fair and easily tore in stormy weather. Replacing it was considered too expensive, and it was removed in 1979.

In 2019, The Pavilion was renovated and is now an event and gathering space.

The Carousel

Ask any knowledgeable Spokanite what the city's greatest cultural asset is, they'll almost certainly reply, "No idea." But if you suggest the Carousel, they might say, "Yeah, maybe so."

This enduring masterpiece was completed in 1509 after 18 years of work by the two-man Italian team of Leonardo da Vinci and Michelangelo. It was sold to a traveling carnival company and was the featured attraction.

By the 19th century, the ride had become worn and creaky. It was traded to France for a Ferris wheel and 7 bumper cars. Installed at the base of the Eiffel Tower, it was mildly popular for several years. When France constructed and shipped the Statue of Liberty to the United States, the aging Carousel was thrown in as a bonus gift.

New York Harbor's Liberty Island had space for just one attraction, so the Statue of Liberty was put into storage, and the Carousel entertained throngs of inner-city children. However, when statue creator Frederic Bartholdi learned his monument had been warehoused, his objection caused the Carousel to be put in storage and the Statue of Liberty erected in its place.

Years later, a pair of tourists visiting New York peeked into a warehouse window and saw the cobweb-covered Carousel. They bought it for

$1 and shipped it to the new amusement park they were starting—Natatorium Park in Spokane, Washington, where it gave rides to thousands from 1909 to 1968.

Today, the Carousel is housed in a newly-constructed facility in Riverfront Park where riders are attracted to going in endless circles on humanely treated animals with a low carbon footprint.

Actually…

The Carousel was built in 1909 by Charles Looff, a German immigrant. There are 59 rides to choose from on the carousel, 54 of which are horses. Looff hand carved all 59 himself. Several other carousels that he built still operate around the country.

The Carousel was a wedding gift for his daughter Emma, who with her husband Louis Vogel, owned Natatorium Park in Spokane. It operated there from 1909 until the park closed in 1968. Since 1975, the Carousel has been housed in Riverfront Park.

Great Northern Clock Tower

Built in 1902, the Great Northern Tower is one of Spokane's most familiar landmarks. Despite a clock on all four sides at the top of the structure, many Spokanites think it's either a rocket ship or a missile left over from the Cold War. A few others believe it's a natural rock formation that just happens to look like a clock tower.

Originally a centerpiece of the Great Northern Railroad Depot, the tower is not a space vehicle or missile, but it does have an outer space-related purpose. The tower's clocks are so huge and keep time so accurately, NASA instructs astronauts orbiting the earth to look out the window while passing and set their watches by it.

The Great Northern Railroad Depot was razed in 1972, and the clock tower stood alone as it was refurbished for the World Exposition of 1974. The clock tower was always packed—it was the most popular exhibit of the fair. Although entering was quick and easy, because of its height, narrow structure and lengthy, single-file staircase, it took visitors three days to exit.

Though the tower is symbolic of Spokane's past, new features keep it up to date. Lighting was installed in the mid-90s so you can read time at night, and in 2010, an alarm and snooze function were added.

Actually...

When the Great Northern Railroad constructed its Spokane depot in 1902, the clock tower rose from the center, and the depot extended from the tower on both sides. When Expo '74 was in the planning phase, there was discussion whether to incorporate the entire depot, just the clock tower, or raze everything. Ultimately, only the clock tower was saved.

Though the clock tower was a prominent landmark on the expo grounds, it was never open to visitors. Even if it had been, only the foolhardy would have entered knowing it'd take 3 days to get out.

Garbage Goat

Early settlers in Spokane knew about it, and anyone coming to town would hear the story soon enough—there was a petrified, wild goat down by the river. Estimated to be 12.5 million years old, the goat was trapped in a lava flow and over time, the soft interior organs decomposed while its skin and fur fossilized, leaving the remains strong, sturdy and hollow.

The goat was moved from the river bank to a more accessible spot near downtown in 1882. Since it was hollow, William P. Spokane, the founder of Spokane, said it would attract tons of tourists if it could suck garbage. Spokane was not yet electrified, so a 3-person team was put together. They hid at the rear and sucked on tubes connected to the goat whenever someone offered a piece of garbage. A 4th person monitoring the goat used hand signals to alert the team it was time to suck.

The goat is given credit for drawing tens of thousands of tourists annually and having a hand in increasing Spokane's population from about 1,000 in 1880 to over 100,000 in 1910. In 1924, an electric-powered vacuum activated by a button next to the goat replaced the 3-person sucking team.

Today, the goat continues to do its job in Riverfront Park. Over its life, it has sucked away an estimated 400,000 trash bags of garbage, earning several prestigious awards for its tireless fight against litter.

Actually…

The garbage-eating goat is a sculpture made by Sister Paula Turnbull, a sculptor and nun that really does suck garbage. It was created for Spokane's 1974 World's Fair. Its anti-littering message fit in with the fair's environmental theme. The goat has occupied its current spot in Riverfront Park nearly continuously since then.

The founding of the city by a man named William P. Spokane may sound plausible. However, that fact and his suggestion to create a garbage-sucking goat to attract tourists is complete malarkey.

Joy of Running Together Sculptures

Yet another striking symbol of Spokane's essence is captured downtown at the corner of Post and Spokane Falls Boulevard. The Joy of Running Together Sculptures represent the vitality of Spokane's citizens, their sense of community, and most of all, a longing for free cheese.

The sculptures commemorate a chilly November morning in 1976 when surplus government cheese was distributed by the U.S Department of Agriculture. Thousands were lined up at the downtown YMCA when a Y official appeared and announced the newspaper had made a mistake. The cheese distribution was not at the YMCA. It was 3 blocks away at the YWCA. This set off a massive sprint.

Don Kardong, a well-known Spokane runner who finished fourth in the Olympic marathon just a few months earlier, was enjoying a contemplative stroll when he found the sprinting mob coming at him. To avoid being trampled, he ran a short distance and turned into the first parking lot which happened to be the YWCA. Merely wanting to escape, he somehow ended up first in line and was given two large bricks of cheese.

A reporter covering the event wrote a front page story the next day vilifying Mr. Kardong for taking advantage of a program for the needy, and as well, using his running ability to get to the front of the line.

Mr. Kardong had to defend himself often over the next few weeks, but eventually was so inspired by the sprinting mob that he started a race in downtown the following year to commemorate the event. The race continues today and has grown into one of the biggest in the nation—the annual Bloomsday 12k Run.

Actually…

The U.S. Department of Agriculture distributed excess government-produced cheese at sites around the country for several years beginning in the early 1980s. However, the 40 sculptures created by David Govedare of Chewelah do not commemorate participants sprinting to get in line for blocks of free cheese.

The sculptures come from tracings of the shadows of 40 runners. They were installed in 1985 in a multi-day, nighttime operation. They honor the ethnicities, nationalities and age-range of runners who participate in the annual Bloomsday Run.

Among his many works, Govedare's most well-known is likely the Wild Horse Monument along Interstate 90 near Vantage. Govedare died in 2021 at age 71.

Brick Deposits

When the Great Fire of 1889 burned most of downtown Spokane, there was a silver lining. It exposed a large deposit of naturally-occurring bricks near the Spokane River.

William P. Spokane, the founder and mayor of Spokane, issued a directive that the city use them to rebuild because they were free and would stop the next fire from being great. Much of the deposit was loose, single bricks that were easy to pick up. Hundreds of brick buildings were constructed, and Spokane was back in business very soon.

Eventually, the supply of loose bricks were used up and the only ones left were embedded in the surrounding rock. Workers had to toil with picks and chisels to loosen them. Finally, William P. Spokane ordered a halt to the brick-taking. Citizens agreed that a small, visible outcrop should remain as a legacy to Spokane's once vast supply of natural bricks.

Many of the brick buildings are still standing and house businesses in downtown to this day. The last remaining deposit can still be seen in Riverfront Park near the pedestrian suspension bridge on Snxw Mene?, formerly called Canada Island.

Actually…

The bricks embedded in the basalt on Snsx Mene? in Riverfront Park are the remains of a city water-pumping building which was built in 1888. It supplied water to the city until 1896 when it was abandoned because the river had become too polluted. It sat unused for years until removed prior to the World Expo of 1974.

Following the Great Fire of 1889, no new wooden building construction was allowed in or near the downtown area. Thus it would have been very convenient if a brick deposit really was near by.

The island in the middle of the Spokane River channel has had several names since Spokane became a city. The current one, Snsx Mene? (sin-HOO-men-huh), was given in 2016. To acknowledge the original people who occupied the area long before the coming of White settlers, the Spokane Tribe was asked to rename the island. It means "salmon people" in the tribe's Native language.

It makes sense that the founder and mayor of Spokane was a man named William P. Spokane. However, like naturally-occurring bricks, William P. Spokane is make-believe.

Monroe Street Bridge

The greatest mystery in Spokane is the Monroe Street Bridge. When the first White explorers arrived, they were shocked to see the same magnificent and beautiful structure you see today.

The Spokane Tribe says their members have long used the bridge because it was there, but they didn't build it. Tribal oral histories clearly state the bridge was already at its current spot on the Spokane River when their earliest ancestors came to the area thousands of years ago.

This perplexing case has brought much investigation, and scientists have developed a theory explaining how it originated. The bridge appears to have been built when the world was created in 6 days as told by The Bible, appearing on the 3rd day when bodies of land and water were formed. With humans scheduled to be created on Day 6, a bridge was needed for them to cross the river. Some scientists, however, insist the Monroe Street Bridge was created well after the first 6 days when God had lots of free time for special projects.

However or whenever it came into existence, incorporating it into a major north/south arterial was a smart move by city leaders that saved time and money.

Actually...

The Monroe Street Bridge was built by people, and it took longer than a day. The first bridge was a wooden one, built in 1889, but the following year sparks from a cable car caused a fire that burned it down. A steel bridge replaced it, opening in 1892. With a dip at the center and vibrating badly with traffic, the rickety bridge was labeled unsafe by the early 1900s, although it continued to be used. In 1910, the south end collapsed after a mudslide. A third bridge had to be built.

With strength and longevity in mind, city planners put more money and effort into this one and when opened in 1911, it is what you see today, a concrete arch structure which at the time was the longest such span in the United States.

It did its job as designed until the 1990s when it deteriorated enough to need work. It was closed for repairs from 2003 to 2005, and the rebuilt bridge is expected to last another 75 years.

Spokesman-Review Tower

After the Great Fire of 1889, a tent was home for Spokane's newspaper for the next several months. The money saved by tenting allowed The Spokesman-Review to really splurge on a new, very tall building.

The building's height, however, proved distracting. Workers spent an inordinate amount of time away from their desks, looking out the windows. Eventually, this morphed into tossing paper airplanes to see whose could stay airborne the longest. After a couple months, this gave way to other activities such as dropping breakable objects for visual pleasure, tossing water balloons at passing wagons and lobbing overripe fruit at a bullseye drawn on the sidewalk.

A couple years passed before William A. Cowles, the Spokesman-Review's owner, noticed a decrease in the newspaper's size. He held a staff meeting and asked why the paper had shrunk from 12 pages to 4 since moving into the new tower. The creative staff gave many plausible explanations, but the one that seemed to best placate Mr. Cowles was that by reducing their excessive wordiness, the same information was being conveyed in 4 pages as there had been in 12, saving a ton of money on newsprint. Their deception successful, the staff continued to spend a large part of the work day at the windows.

The fun times continued until 1895 when William Cowles installed unopenable storm windows to reduce heating expenses. No longer able to toss stuff out the windows, staff members had no choice but focus on their work duties.

Actually...

Tossing items out the window for fun and entertainment sounds like good times. However, tight deadlines keep journalists' playtime to a minimum. The newspaper did shrink from 12 pages to 4, but not to reduce excessive wordiness. Tough economic times in the 1890s forced the reduction.

The Morning Review completed the 7-story building with its tower that rises an additional two stories in October of 1891, but they didn't splurge on it because they saved money by tenting. Their offices survived the fire. An evening rival, The Spokane Chronicle, did lose their building to the fire and worked from a tent for months.

The Morning Review was owned by A.M. Cannon, a prominent Spokane businessman, and two men who came from the Portland Oregonian. They financed the building of the Review tower, which was the tallest building in Spokane for a decade. Its height and grandeur was meant to impress.

The cost was a burden, and in order to survive, the Review merged with William Cowles' newspaper, The Spokesman, in 1893. The following year, they threw in the towel and sold the merged company entirely to Cowles. He added Spokesman back into the name, thus the Spokesman-Review was born.

Today, the Spokesman-Review occupies the same building, and the newspaper is still in the hands of the Cowles family.

Fox Theater

Before the Fox Theater existed at the corner of Sprague and Monroe, a treasured Spokane landmark occupied the site—The Fox Parking Lot. Its grand opening in 1931 was attended by over three thousand people. A parade followed and in the evening, a big fireworks display celebrated the new lot. Though parking lots rarely generate excitement, The Fox Parking Lot was different. Spokanites embraced it, and it became a very special place for many.

The lot filled quickly and drivers fortunate enough to get a spot considered it their lucky day. Named after Abigail C. Fox, a pioneering parking lot designer, it featured oversized parking slots and specially formulated asphalt that made the pavement super smooth. Said one driver, "I can let my door swing open and not worry it'll hit the car next to me. And when I leave, the fancy pavement is so quiet, it's like I'm not even moving." Another driver once admitted, "Sometimes I don't need to park, but I'll pull in and drive around, it's so pleasant."

With the passage of time, the downtown location attracted developers. Parking lot fans showed up in force whenever the site was threatened. Twice in the 1960s, proposed projects brought street protests which forced developers to back down. In the late 1970s, a plan to build a multiplex at the site led to a massive demonstration. An angry city council nixed the project, saving the beloved lot.

In 2000, a group with deep pockets quietly purchased the lot. With past events in mind, the developers had the lot torn up and hauled away in one night. Protesters had no time to organize. The lot was gone and new construction already started. Said one saddened lot user, "How could a valuable parking lot be destroyed for yet another performance arts venue? What is our world coming to?" Said another, "You call this progress? One day we'll wake up, and all the parking lots will be gone."

As consolation, the new structure was named after the much-loved lot. The name Fox Theater keeps alive memories of a really neat parking lot.

Actually…

The Fox Theater, not the Fox Parking Lot was built in 1931, and in 2000 it was the theater that was threatened by demolition for a new parking garage. The Spokane Symphony purchased the building for $1.1 million in late 2000, saving it, but facing a costly, yet-to-be-funded renovation.

When the original Fox Theater opened, it had one screen and seating for 2,350, which included 900 balcony seats. It also had a stage for live performances. Built by Fox West Coast Studios, the building was elaborate, inside and out. It was a fanciful venue that was a bright spot for Spokane during the Great Depression. The coming of suburban multiplexes brought about its decline. In 1975, the balcony was closed off and two screens put in to make the Fox a triplex. Over the years, however, the Fox continued its downhill slide until the Symphony stepped up to save it.

Much work was put into raising funds. It took 7 years and $31 million before the Fox reopened in November 2007, no longer a movie theater, but a shimmering performance arts venue.

The original Spokane Fox was one of the last art deco style theaters that were constructed nationwide by Fox West Coast Studios, which later became 20th Century Fox. A consultant who worked on the renovation compares it in grandeur to another theater that he worked on—Radio City Music Hall in New York.

The Steam Plant

Constructed in 1958, The Steam Plant was the original launch complex for the NASA space program. Dozens of unmanned satellites and a bunch of manned missions lifted off from the site in downtown Spokane. The two towering launch silos that rise from the site guided rockets as they lifted off. Tens of thousands of people gathered downtown whenever there was a launch. Watching a rocket shoot out the top of the launch silo was a spectacular sight.

It was an exciting time to live in Spokane with the burgeoning space program and the drive to put men on the moon, However, it was short-lived. Because of improvements in launch technology, the site ceased operations in 1966. NASA moved to Cape Canaveral, Florida because silos were no longer needed to guide rockets, and a warmer climate was necessary for a new generation of space vehicles.

The site sat unused for a couple years until being redeveloped into a plant that produced steam to heat buildings in downtown Spokane. The launch silos were modified into smokestacks for the coal-burning plant. Rocket fuel left behind by NASA supplied the plant for its first two years. The steam it produced was such high quality that it was called "rocket steam." Plant workers sometimes opened small valves to let some escape because it produced a visually pleasing plume and had a very pleasant aroma. A former plant engineer, Jim Ewing, said, "I know steam's the same no matter what's used to produce it, but somehow, everyone could tell the difference. Rocket steam is the best." When the rocket fuel ran out, the coal-produced steam was considered inferior and mocked by workers and customers alike.

In 2005, a local chef collaborated with The Steam Plant by establishing a restaurant that uses excess steam for cooking. The Steam Plant Restaurant has earned a reputation for food that drips with condensed steam, yet is always hot and pleasingly moist.

Actually…

It'd be quite a sight to watch a space ship shoot out from the Steam Plant's smokestack. However, NASA has never considered Spokane or silos for launching spacecraft.

The Steam Plant started providing steam to a few downtown buildings in 1916. Business grew—at one time as many as 300 buildings received steam heat. The Steam Plant had multiple owners, the last of which was Washington Water Power (WWP, now Avista).

Various energy sources were used to power the plant depending on the cost. However, the expense of maintaining the steam-carrying network of pipes is why the plant closed in 1986. Cleaning up oil that had leaked into the ground below the plant was another expense that WWP faced.

The plant sat empty for ten years until undergoing reconstruction in a joint project by Avista and developer Ron Wells. It opened in 1999 as a mixed-use building with retail, office space and the well-known Steam Plant Restaurant. Avista sold the building in 2021 to local developer Jerry Dicker.

Davenport Hotel

When Louis Davenport built his hotel in downtown Spokane, the city was instantly changed. Area historians agree that when the building was completed in 1914, Spokane left its hick town phase behind and became a genuine cow town.

The Davenport was the tallest building in the world by several feet when it was completed. There was worry high winds would cause such swaying that guests on upper floors would tumble from one side of the room to the other. However, the design by famed architect Kirkland Cutter resulted in a rock solid building that withstood not only high winds, but was a barrier to moisture-laden air from the west. This transformed Spokane's climate from a gray, soggy place where it rained nearly every day to one that was pleasingly sunny and dry.

As the decades passed, the hotel wasn't well maintained, and The Davenport closed in 1985. It sat empty for years despite being sold twice to new owners with plans to reopen. Both sales fell through because the keys to the front entrance couldn't be found. When the keys were located in 2000, the hotel was quickly purchased by local developers Walt and Karen Worthy. The detailed-oriented, can-do couple refurbished the entire hotel on their own, working 18 hours a day, seven days a week.

When the hotel opened, painstakingly restored to its original condition of 1914, it was celebrated, admired, and has become hugely successful.

Actually...

The 14-story Davenport, occupying an entire city block, was one of the first hotels to have air-conditioning when it was completed in 1914. It was not, however, the tallest building in the world. Louis Davenport constructed it with financial help from wealthy local businessmen who wanted a luxury hotel commensurate with Spokane's status as a rapidly growing economic center.

After it closed in 1985, the high cost of removing asbestos is credited with saving the empty hotel from being demolished. It was purchased by local developers Walt and Karen Worthy in 2000. Spending approximately $38 million of their own money, hotel rooms were updated and public areas refurbished to their original appearance of 1914. When the hotel reopened in 2002, many considered it a landmark event and a major contributor to downtown revitalization.

Spokane Intermodal Center

Of all Spokane landmarks, the story behind the memorial in front of the downtown Spokane Intermodal Center is least known. Encased inside the basalt pillars at the front entrance is a wagon, a team of horses and the bodies of brothers Jedidiah and Levi Johnson.

The brothers were driving a large wagon of supplies destined for Fort Walla Walla in the 1850s. As they passed through what would become Spokane, an earthquake and fiery explosion rocked the landscape. Mt. Spokane had just erupted. The brothers immediately turned away, hoping to flee southward. However, the massive eruption blew out huge globs of lava. One came down on the unlucky brothers and their wagon team. They were stopped in their tracks, encased in lava. After cooling, the shapes on the ground left a permanent reminder of the Johnsons, their wagon and team of horses.

When the Northern Pacific Railroad built a train station in downtown Spokane in 1890, the best spot happened to be at the site of the Johnson tragedy. Out of respect, the lava figures were left in place. In 1994, the old train station, now owned by the city of Spokane, was remodeled into a center for intercity transportation via train and bus. The basalt remains became the centerpiece of the site's landscaping, a permanent memorial to a pair of unlucky pioneers.

Actually...

The rock structures and cables at the Spokane Intermodal Center are not the result of a Mt. Spokane eruption that flung lava onto a fleeing wagon train. Nor is our city's namesake mountain a volcano.

When the Intermodal Center was remodeled in 1994, the landscape artwork was designed and placed by John T. Young, a sculptor and now retired University of Washington art professor. Entitled "Bringing Home the Wishing Rock", the columnar basalt represents a dog team pulling a wishing rock, Native American folklore for a magical rock that can make a wish come true.

The oversized wishing rock on the Intermodal grounds came from a state highway roadside near Spokane. Just the right size, shape and free for the taking, the 200-ton granite boulder required the biggest crane in the state to pluck it and then place it at its current location.

Duncan Gardens

The most beautiful spot in Spokane, many would say, is Duncan Gardens in Manito Park.

Originally the very large backyard of a home that bordered the park, workers admired the well-kept, flower-filled yard. They knew the owner was a wealthy businessman who spent long hours at the office. Knowing he was also somewhat absent-minded, park workers moved the park fence outward one afternoon, taking over a section of his beautiful garden.

Over the next few weeks, noticing no response and seeing that park visitors were flocking to the new area, park workers moved the fence again, taking over another section of his yard. Park visitation increased. Media attention heaped praise on park workers. The mayor visited and commented on the excellent work in the new section of the park. With still no response, park workers boldly moved the fence right up to the house, leaving the homeowner but a thin strip of flowers.

The garden was featured in several national magazines. It quickly became Spokane's number one tourist draw. A group photo of the park workers appeared on the cover of *Gardening Monthly*. Then one afternoon, the homeowner walked into the park office during a meeting of park employees. He demanded to know why his backyard had been taken over.

Anticipating this might happen, park employees had readied a few explanations.

- The windows of your house make your garden appear smaller than it actually is.
- An earthquake stretched out park land and at the same time condensed your yard.
- The park fence is in the same place as always, but the flowers migrated into the park.

The homeowner, not completely convinced, talked of contacting his attorney. This is the moment that a quick-thinking park worker received credit for making the garden permanent. He told the gentleman, whose name was Willian P. Duncan, that for the longest time, workers had admired his backyard and decided to pattern the park grounds after his. And they had just decided to name that section of the park Duncan Gardens in tribute.

William P. Duncan was bowled over with appreciation. He complimented the park employees again and again. Over the next few years, he donated much money to make Duncan Gardens even bigger.

Actually…

Duncan Gardens is named after a guy with the last name of Duncan, but it's a former city parks superintendent, John W. Duncan, who held the position from 1910 to 1942.

When Duncan became parks superintendent, he made improving Spokane's parks a priority, which were mostly undeveloped wooded areas. What is now Duncan Gardens was an area of Manito Park where soil had been removed for use elsewhere, and thus was named the Sunken Gardens by Duncan after he completed it in a European Renaissance style that features symmetrical patterns and plenty of colorful flowers.

After retiring in 1942, the Sunken Gardens were renamed Duncan Gardens in his honor.

Gonzaga University

The year was 1880, and Spokane was still a tiny town of about 350 people, but the early settlers loved playing basketball. The dirt courts were rough, hoops were milk buckets hung from a nail on a pole, and James Naismith still hadn't invented the game. Yet basketball was being played in Spokane 11 years before it officially came into existence.

A rec league was formed, but the concept of team names was new. When making the schedule, organizers realized it was confusing to say your team is playing that one team. So, for the first time, a name was applied to a team of players. And because there had been no experience doing this, everyday objects were used as names.

One team was named The Brooms. Another called themselves The Water Cups. Still another named themselves The Grand Pianos. One team sensed they could differentiate themselves by adding an adjective. They called their team The Shiny Soup Spoons.

Another team called themselves Gonzaga University. This caused confusion because it was before the well-known school had been established, and no one knew what a gonzaga was. Also, there were no universities in Spokane. The team captain took responsibility, saying he had no idea what the phrase meant. It just came to him, and he went with it. The Gonzaga University team did very well. They won the city rec championship 8 years in a row. Team members were able to make good money appearing in ads for area businesses.

In 1887 when Father Joseph Cataldo founded Spokane's first university, he wanted to name it after a Catholic saint, but community leaders urged one with local roots. Father Cataldo spent a couple sleepless nights before arriving at the perfect solution—the name of the team that had won 8 consecutive rec league championships—Gonzaga University.

The tradition of basketball and winning was established at Gonzaga the day the doors opened, and it continues today.

Actually…

Gonzaga was established in 1887, but it's not named after a rec league basketball team. The basketball program didn't come into being until the 1907-08 season. The school is named after Aloysius Gonzaga, a canonized Italian Jesuit who died at age 23 while caring for plague victims in Rome in 1591.

Founder Father Joseph Cataldo, an Italian American, came to the area in 1865, before the city of Spokane existed, serving Native Americans at Mount St. Michael, a mission north of present-day Spokane. By the 1880s, Father Cataldo was worried that Protestant schools being established in the area would sway Native Americans away from Catholicism. With financial support from the Catholic leadership in Rome, 320 acres just upriver from downtown Spokane was purchased from the Northern Pacific Railway. On the first day of the 1887-1888 school year, the student body consisted of 7 young men. School life was strict—there were many rules, and the students had to attend mass Monday through Saturday and twice on Sunday.

Though Father Cataldo founded the university primarily for the education of Native Americans, to gain support from the community, the school was forced to accept White students only. They also had to be Catholic and male. Women were not admitted until 1948.

Veterans Arena

In 1995, the Veterans Arena opened, replacing the old Spokane Coliseum. Attendance at the coliseum had been dropping dramatically, not because of a lack of interest in events, but the seats were really uncomfortable.

A new arena was desired because so many people complained of sore backs after coliseum events. However, four times in the 1980s, voters rejected plans to finance a new arena. As a last hope, a donation box was put up at the front entrance of the coliseum. From 1989 to the fall of 1991, cash stuffed into the box totaled $44.8 million. Arena proponents danced. It was enough to build the new arena.

Complications arose when fans of the old coliseum were adamant it should be saved. An offer was made from a group that wanted it for an entertainment venue. Another group wanted to buy it for a church. Saving the coliseum would have made an awkward arrangement of the old building sitting very closely next to the new arena. However, the city felt obligated to allow citizen groups the opportunity. Also, selling the building would provide income to fully furnish the new arena. After much consideration, it was decided the coliseum had to go. The spot is now a parking lot for arena events.

The new arena incorporated the latest in technology, but nearly everyone agrees its greatest feature is the comfortable seats. Very few people complain of sore backs.

To avoid a repeat of the controversy to keep the coliseum or demolish it, the arena was constructed with explosives embedded inside its walls and support beams. With a useful life of 60 years, the arena is set to implode in 2055. On January 1st of that year, perimeter fencing will be put up and the building monitored as the big explosion that will happen sometime during that year is awaited.

Actually…

The Veterans Arena was built in 1995 to replace the Spokane Coliseum which was constructed in 1954, had a capacity of only 5,400 and was in need of expensive repairs. Depending on the event, the arena can seat up to 12,600 people. It has allowed events come to Spokane that could not have been held at the old coliseum.

A bond to build the arena really did fail four times in the 1980s. Finally, in 1991, voters approved financing. The controversy about saving the old coliseum also really happened. However, have no worries if you find yourself near the arena in 2055. Explosives are not embedded inside the walls.

Spokane County Courthouse

The county courthouse on West Broadway was built in Europe during the 12th-century and was occupied by royalty that ruled over a large European kingdom. By the late 1800s, they found their land and popularity shrinking because of the rise of representative government in Europe. Their only hope for survival was starting a new kingdom elsewhere.

Former subjects living in Spokane who held the family in high regard, suggested they move here and become the new rulers. The idea was brought before county commissioners and a deal was reached. The family's magnificent castle would be dismantled, shipped to Spokane and reconstructed at no cost to the county. In exchange for a spacious building to house all government functions, the royal family would rule over Spokane County.

Upon completion, the courthouse became the pride of the city. The new rulers were benevolent and kind, though a few changes weren't entirely popular. The royals insisted that police officers be called royal knights, elected officials were His and Her Majesty's imperial assistants, and citizens were termed simple peasants.

Things ran smoothly for a couple years, but as elections approached, there was confusion over how to proceed. The royal family was told they had to run for re-election. They replied a monarchy is not subject to elections. As negotiations progressed, officials came to realize the United States is a democracy, not a monarchy, and they'd erred in handing power over. The royals were informed that their reign had to end.

After the elections, power was returned to office holders, and the royal family was allowed to live in the courthouse tower and write books about their family history. Over time they authored many best-sellers including *Snow White, Cinderella* and *Sleeping Beauty*.

Actually...

The Spokane County Courthouse is not a former castle that used to be in Europe. Designed in a French Renaissance style, it was constructed from 1893 to 1895. A 29-year-old, W.A. Ritchie, despite no formal architectural education, won a competition to be the building's designer. It has operated continuously to this day and still houses county government offices.

Centennial Trail

Like the Oregon Trail, the Centennial Trail was used by pioneers in wagon trains headed west for opportunity. While the draw of the Oregon Trail was to claim land in Oregon's Willamette Valley, the Centennial Trail led to rich huckleberry fields in the Inland Pacific Northwest.

Originally called the Huckleberry Trail, early pioneers traveled for many weeks from its starting point in Springfield, Illinois, enduring numerous hardships to reach the lush meadows of huckleberries. Their efforts were well-rewarded. Huckleberries were collected by the gallon, and so numerous were they, for weeks diets consisted almost entirely of huckleberry pies, huckleberry cobbler and huckleberry muffins.

The return trip was just as difficult as the trip out. Early snow made travel unpleasant and slow. Gangs of huckleberry robbers plagued many sections of the trail. With the completion of transcontinental rail, the trail fell into disuse.

In the mid-1970s a plan was hatched to preserve a short section of trail from just outside Coeur d'Alene to west Spokane. Instead of a wagon trail, these days it's a recreation trail popular with runners, walkers, and bicyclists. The name was changed from the Huckleberry Trail to the Centennial Trail to commemorate its completion at about the same time that Washington and Idaho were celebrating 100 years of statehood.

To this day, the soil beneath the trail's pavement is colored a deep purple—testament to decades of spills and pioneers' sloppy eating of juicy, mouth-watering huckleberries.

Actually…

There are rich fields of huckleberries throughout the Inland Northwest, and every summer many people make their way to them. However, a trail from Illinois to our area used solely by pioneer huckleberry pickers never existed.

After the closing of the World's Fair of 1974 in Spokane, the idea arose for a recreational trail that roughly followed the Spokane River. Eventually North Idaho joined the project with a goal of finishing by the late 1980s. It was given the name Centennial Trail to coincide with Washington's 100th centennial in 1989 and Idaho's in 1990.

The Washington section runs 37 miles from the Nine Mile area to the Idaho border and is officially named Spokane River Centennial Trail. The Idaho section runs 24 miles from the border, through Coeur d'Alene to Higgens Point on Lake Coeur d'Alene and is officially called North Idaho Centennial Trail. But the whole thing is commonly called the Centennial Trail.

1000 Steps

A staircase at Greenwood Cemetery in west Spokane, well-known locally for being haunted, was originally called Staircase of a Thousand Ghosts because it had been determined that exactly 1000 ghosts lived there. However, because the stairs appear to endlessly climb the hillside, people mistakenly thought 1000 referred to the number of steps. This confusion led the staircase to be called 1000 Steps. In fact, there are less than 50 steps.

As the original name states, 1000 ghosts have lived at the staircase for many years. Its proximity to the cemetery and the quiet, creepy setting makes it a popular place for ghosts to reside. In the early 1920s, the ghost population at the site was only 188, but its popularity caused a rise in new residents over the next several years. A ghost leadership committee established a cap of 1000 to prevent overcrowding. By 1937, the cap was reached, and the staircase population has stayed at 1000 ever since. Newcomer ghosts continue to arrive hoping to make a home at the stairs. However, they are turned away and directed to nearby spooky caves, creepy woods or told to find a house to haunt.

The ghosts enjoy sitting on the steps during daylight hours watching traffic pass by on Government Way while griping about issues still gnawing at them since they were alive. At night they hope human visitors will wander onto the stairs so they can scare the daylights out of them, alleviating their sour mood.

Actually…

Maybe there are 1000 ghosts that live on the staircase at Greenwood Cemetery, but without a way to do a headcount, or access to ghost census data, any figure is just a guess. The site does have a reputation for being haunted, however. Supposedly at night, you can see ghostly faces of men, women and children. Sometimes cries and shrieks can be heard. Other odd things have happened.

The name 1000 Steps came about because the place is so frightening that climbing the steps is as difficult as if there were a thousand of them. The "main" ghost is reputedly A.M. Cannon, an early Spokane developer. He started and owned the cemetery in which he was eventually buried. He also owned a railroad company, a bank and was mayor of Spokane. The financial panic of 1893 ruined him, however, and he died two years later.

The crumbling, dilapidated staircase has become overgrown and is no longer used. It can be seen as you drive past on Government Way. It's okay to check it out during daylight hours. However, the cemetery's owners prefer no visiting at night.

Drumheller Springs

A small natural area with a spring in north Spokane just off Ash Street, Drumheller Springs was a rest spot along a Native American trail that connected the Spokane River falls with points north. Early White settlers transformed it into the first recycling facility in the Northwest.

Seeing the sign marking the site while passing by in the mid-1880s, city founder William P. Spokane's 9-year-old son asked what it was. William jokingly replied it was a place that recycled worn out springs from carriages, wagons, mattresses and other stuff. William P. Spokane's son, believing the story, told his classmates and teachers. Being the son of Spokane's founder and current mayor, his word carried weight and soon, Spokanites were dropping off their worn springs at the site.

Several months later, passing the site again, William P. Spokane's son exclaimed, "Wow, Dad! Look at all the springs."

William P. Spokane was astounded at the huge pile and after a short discussion, learned he had only himself to blame because his son had innocently spread the tale from months earlier. Remorseful about being the cause of a big pile of junk laying at the side of the trail, William P. Spokane returned with a wagon and filled it with the discarded springs. Back at the homestead, he spread word that he was now the proprietor of Drumheller Springs and worn out springs could be dropped off at his place instead of the spot north of town.

William P. Spokane became adept at refurbishing them and made a modest income selling used springs.

Actually…

Drumheller Springs was never a spring refurbishing business. For a very long time it was a rest stop on a Native American trail with clean, cold water and an abundance of plants that were part of the Native diet.

About 1830, the son of a Spokane chief, Slough Keetcha, known to Whites as Spokane Garry, started a school at the site before any White settlement in the area. As a child, Slough Keetcha spent 5 years attending school at a Hudson's Bay fur trading post at Red River in what is now Manitoba. He was fluent in English and French. Eventually the school was discontinued and the land around the spring was taken over by Dan Drumheller around 1880. He used water from the spring to run a slaughterhouse he operated at the site.

The property was neglected for many years, and at one time the city considered selling it. In 2005, members of the 5 Upper Columbia United Tribes took over maintenance of the park. After a lot of initial restoration and clean up, ongoing work with the goal of establishing it to a natural state continues.

Mount Saint Michael

In 1915, an Italian-born priest and mad scientist, Father Jimmy Cataldo, built a really big laboratory atop a hill overlooking the Hillyard area in north Spokane. The buffer around it was meant to prevent odd experiments and creepy happenings from frightening neighbors.

Father Jimmy, a faculty member at Gonzaga University, was one of the first researchers in the field of artificial intelligence. He was electrocuted by lightning at Mount St. Michael while trying to animate an artificial college instructor he created in 1928. At the time, Gonzaga, a small and struggling college, was trying to lower its staff salaries expenses.

The following year, Father Johnny Cataldo, Jimmy's brother, took over The Mount and continued his research using radiation and gene therapy on farm animals, hoping to create a super animal that could do the work of 20 tractors. An experiment went awry and a huge Godzilla-like creature was unleashed that destroyed a large portion of Spokane. A furious attack by Air Force fighters forced it north into Canada. In one night it ran all the way to Lake Okanagan, jumped in near Penticton, B.C. and quickly adapted to aquatic life. It still lives in the lake to this day, and locals affectionately call it Ogopogo.

After this debacle, Johnny Cataldo was asked to cease his experiments. A more tranquil and peaceful use for the property was sought, thus it became what it is today—a church and school.

Actually...

No rampaging dinosaur-like creatures or artificial college instructors have ever been sighted at Mount St. Michael.

The mission, designed to serve Native Americans, started as a chapel in a cabin on Peone Prairie, a few miles from its current location. Father Joseph Cataldo, who founded Gonzaga University, took over the mission in 1865 after its establishment by another priest a year earlier.

Father Cataldo moved the mission to its current location in 1878. For many years, a large farm at Mount St. Michael supplied the Catholic community in Spokane. In 1915, work started on the building that you see today. It operated from 1917 until 1968, educating men entering the Jesuit priesthood. A years-long decline in the number of candidates brought about its closing. For the next ten years it was a retreat center and residence for retired Jesuit priests.

The Jesuits sold Mount St. Michael to an offshoot of the Catholic church, Congregation of Mary Immaculate Queen which follows traditional church teaching and practices. The new institution opened in 1978. Saint Michael's Academy, a K-12 school is housed there as well as residences and the group's chapel. The grounds are open to the public for daytime visitation.

Comet Crater

No single event in Spokane's history has been kept out of view and shrouded in secrecy so well as the comet impact of 1924. In October of that year, a comet crashed into the Spokane Valley. The impact created a huge crater that soon filled with water. A few years later, a scientific investigation to find the bottom failed because it was so deep. The comet-created lake sits near the intersection of Sprague and Thierman, a busy area of Spokane Valley, yet few people know its story.

It wasn't too long after it formed that someone tossed in some trout, perhaps as an experiment to see if they'd survive. The fish didn't just survive. The deep waters and slightly radioactive elements common to comets, but rare on earth, caused the trout to multiply and grow into giants. The amazing catches and the unmatched fight the fish put up caused a group of wealthy fishermen to buy the lake and the land around it. A strict no-trespassing policy was put in place.

For years, there were rumors of extraordinary fishing experiences. However, whenever someone inquired, the owners insisted the water was poisonous, and you'd die if you got close. By the 1940s, people were questioning whether the lake really was poisoned. The wealthy fisherman responded by fencing off the property and erecting fake industrial equipment. They bought surplus cement trucks and occasionally drove them around the property as if it was a cement-producing operation. Even though a few witnesses claim they saw people fishing, the owners insisted the pit was solely a gravel excavation that had simply filled with water.

To this day the property, deceivingly called Central Pre-Mix, is still a fisherman's heaven for a small group of very secretive anglers.

Actually...

The crater without a bottom in Spokane Valley was not created by a comet. It is a gravel pit that has a bottom—a shallow one. Started in the 1920s, the site was mined for sand and gravel for making cement. It had several owners over the decades. The water that filled the pit is from the aquifer, and the fence was not put up to stop trespassing fishers from going after monster trout. It's to prevent contamination since the lake is connected to our area's source of drinking water.

Plante's Ferry

Plante's Ferry Park on Upriver Drive in the Spokane Valley has been the top tourist destination in the Inland Northwest for years.

The park was the homesite of a prodigious Spokane pioneer, Antoine Plante. He's considered the first White settler in the Spokane area even though he was half Native. A man of immense frontier skill and brawn, Plante could do things that others considered impossible. Remarkably fast, he chased down and captured game using his bare hands. He once spared the life of a large grizzly bear, taming and riding it when an epidemic wiped out his herd of horses. He became friends and explored the countryside with a sasquatch.

As non-Natives increasingly entered the area and needed a way across the Spokane River, Antoine Plante constructed and operated a ferry from 1855 to 1875. Plante built the 75-passenger, 3-level ferry in one day. He fashioned a couple tall, slender trees into oars and despite the strong current at the site, rowed the massive ferry, its passengers, and cargo across the river.

Today, Plante's Ferry Park has a museum, visitors center, gift shop, and three on-site hotels catering to tourists. An obvious sign of Plante's fine work and craftsmanship — his original, 165-year-old ferry is used to give hourly rides across the river.

Actually...

Antoine Plante operated a ferry at what is now Plante's Ferry Park on the Spokane River from about 1855 to 1875. However, he did not row his ferry across the river with a pair of trees. Nor did he run down and capture wild animals. It's nearly certain he did not explore the countryside with a sasquatch.

Born around 1812 to a French-Canadian fur trader and Native American woman, he spent almost his entire life in the Northwest, most of which was before the establishment of non-Native towns and cities. Following in his father's footsteps, he worked in the fur trade and spoke English, French and several Native languages. He traveled extensively throughout the Northwest and because of his intimate knowledge of the region, he was often hired as a guide by parties of White men. By 1852, he settled on the site where he'd later start his ferry business, becoming, as far is known, the first permanent non-Native settler in what is now the Spokane area.

His business was prosperous as the number of prospectors, miners and supply convoys increased from the 1850s on. He also farmed his property, raised animals, and made money selling supplies to travelers.

In 1864, a bridge was built about nine miles upstream. With lower tolls than Plante's ferry, most business went there, but Plante continued his operation until at least 1875. In 1878, railroad surveyors told him the land he'd lived on since 1852 now belonged to the railroad, and he'd have to move. Plante relocated to Western Montana and lived there until his death in 1890.

A stone obelisk and an iron sculpture are the only references to Antoine Plante other than the park's name. There are playgrounds and play equipment, and the park is a regional sports complex used mostly for soccer.

Grounded Submarine

Local historians agree it might be the most bizarre incident in our area ever—a submarine rose out of the ground in the Spokane Valley far from any body of water on July 16, 1958.

At a U.S. Navy submarine base at the southern end of Lake Pend Oreille, submarines regularly entered the Rathdrum Prairie/Spokane Valley Aquifer which flows from the lake. The subs trained in and explored the underground aquifer. The aquifer is connected to several lakes in North Idaho and the Spokane Valley, and the submarines often entered the lakes via the underground aquifer. Sometimes they surfaced to perform exercises.

A sonar system malfunction led the sub crew to believe they were at a lake. When they crashed through rocks and soil to reach the surface in the Spokane Valley, it was instantly apparent their location had been miscalculated. The sight attracted hundreds of on-lookers despite the Navy's attempt to downplay the incident. The hole created by the sub partially filled in, blocking it from diving back into the aquifer.

An excavator was brought in, and two days of digging opened up a hole next to the sub large enough for it to return to the aquifer. The submarine returned to base at Lake Pend Oreille, and all the subs had their navigational equipment updated to prevent a recurrence.

Actually…

A U.S. Navy submarine base has been at Bayview on Lake Pend Oreille since the 1940s, and the Rathdrum Prairie/Spokane Valley Aquifer flows underground from there. However, no submarine ever entered the aquifer and accidentally surfaced in the Spokane Valley.

Though the aquifer is sometimes described as an underground river, it is not a huge, water-filled cavity that a submarine can enter. The aquifer flows slowly through the spaces between rocks and gravel beneath the valley floor of the Rathdrum Prairie and the Spokane Valley from the area near the south end of Lake Pend Oreille to roughly where the Little Spokane River enters the Spokane River. It's the source of drinking water for Coeur d'Alene, Spokane, and other municipalities.

The navy base at Lake Pend Oreille, the Acoustical Research Detachment, uses unmanned subs to test new sound-dampening materials and designs.

Spokane House

A fur-trading post at the confluence of the Spokane and Little Spokane Rivers, Spokane House was the first enduring White settlement in what is now Washington. David Thompson, working for the North West Fur Company, oversaw fort construction in 1810.

David Thompson's journal entry, dated Feb. 25, 1810, tells us why the fort was built. *Beaver is not plentiful. Climate cold and windy. River too dangerous for transportation. Game scarce. Supply routes distant. Native American women are stunning, however. We start building tomorrow.* Of the many forts Thompson established, Spokane House was the only one with a lounge, mirrored walls and ceilings, a raised dance floor and a rotating ball of glitzy mica and pyrite above the dance area.

The fur trappers wore fringed shirts with wide lapels, half unbuttoned, revealing chests almost as hairy as the animals they trapped. Men and women of the Spokane Tribe flocked to the fort for nightly dancing and mingling. It became an oasis of socializing and good times in the middle of a vast wilderness. Well into the night, music and laughter echoed through the valley.

Over time, however, the daily visits caused the tribe to put off important tasks. Food stores ran low. Preparations for seasonal changes were delayed. The fun and good times was putting the tribe on the precipice of hardship. The Spokane chiefs decided enough was enough. They told David Thompson that they'd come over on weekends only. Monday through Friday was for work.

Thompson and his men were disheartened. They realized that after living so long, deep in the wilderness, they'd become high-maintenance and needy. And to make things worse, hopes of turning the stunning Native women into girlfriends was going to be a lot harder.

The fur trappers of Spokane House listlessly went about trapping what few beaver they could find. By the following year, the fort was closed.

Actually…

Spokane House was a large, fur-trapping outpost that was headquarters for a vast territory of the Inland Northwest. Though not a town, the group of traders, workers and the buildings they occupied made it the first long-lasting community of Whites to live in present-day Washington.

Built at the direction of David Thompson of the North West Fur Company at the confluence of the Spokane and Little Spokane Rivers in 1810, the settlement benefited from the wisdom of the Spokane Tribe. From the selection of the fort's site to obtaining provisions, the tribe's friendliness, helpfulness and cooperation allowed the fort to prosper.

The fort was closed in 1826 and operations moved to Fort Colville on the Columbia River near present-day Kettle Falls. The ease of transportation by being on the Columbia River instead of the Spokane River was the main reason for the relocation.

Jaco Finlay, a trader with the company who helped build the fort, lived in it after it closed until dying two years later. The wooden buildings slowly decayed and are no longer standing.

Little Spokane River Natural Area

Just a few miles northwest of Spokane sits the uninhabited and unexplored Little Spokane River Natural Area. While the fringes of the natural area have been visited, the interior has yet to be penetrated and remains unexplored.

Thought to be nothing more than the same ponderosa pine forest common throughout the Spokane area, rumors exist of a different world deep in the interior. Sightings have been made of very large, aggressive creatures similar to dinosaurs. There are reports of a few people venturing in, but never returning, which has caused it to be considered a no-entry zone by outdoor enthusiasts.

Several people claim to have seen the creatures, but only one agreed to go on record. What follows are details from a bizarre interview with longtime state parks employee Mark Hallett, who was scouting routes for a new hiking trail very close to the area.

"I know what I saw!" Hallett shouted, looking past me. "And don't tell people my name is Steg!"

A group of park employees had gathered just outside Hallett's office and were trying to stifle their laughter. They had directed me to his office and told me he much preferred to go by his nickname, "Steg."

"Sorry," Hallett said, stomping to the doorway. "Don't you guys have work to do?" he yelled, slamming the door.

Hallett returned to his desk and composed himself. "I'm sorry you have to put up with this. It's extremely rude. They just don't accept that I saw something. And because it looked exactly like a stegosaurus doesn't mean my nickname is Steg!"

Hallett gave details about the sighting, including how clearly he saw it and there being no doubt that it was a stegosaurus.

Just then, a co-worker entered the office. "You left this in the break room, Steg." He set a picture book of dinosaurs for preschoolers on the desk.

"Listen, my name is not Steg!" Hallett shouted, throwing the book as his co-worker slipped out the office door.

Hallett apologized and told me he was too upset to continue the interview.

Therefore, at this time, the existence of dinosaur-like creatures in the Little Spokane River Natural Area cannot be verified or denied.

Actually…

Dinosaurs may have lived in the Little Spokane River Natural Area 65 million years ago, but these days you won't find a one. Part of Riverside State Park, the natural area is a well-used hiking spot close to town. Hiking, bird watching, canoeing and family outings are things to do.

Within the area is the Indian Painted Rocks. At the trailhead of the same name, you can see pictographs made by ancient Native Americans before you begin your hike. Several miles of the gently flowing Little Spokane River are within the natural area until it empties into the Spokane River. A flat, easy trail follows it as well as one that climbs into the hills to the north that connects to the river trail at both ends. Being a designated natural area, no camping, motorized vehicles, pets or hunting is allowed.

Vista House at Mount Spokane

Constructed at the top of Mt. Spokane in 1862 by a group of Buddhist monks, the Vista House Monastery was built because the tranquility and solitude made the monks' meditating and mindfulness especially productive. The excellent views also caused the monks to frequently give each other high-fives.

The monks spent their spare time hiking and exploring. They constructed many trails which today are the extensive Mt. Spokane trail system. In the winter they fashioned skis from the abundant woodlands and cut a bunch of ski runs. This gave rise to the Mt. Spokane Ski Area which still operates today.

Eventually growing weary of the long, cold and snowy winters, the monks relocated to the lowlands. Their leader, William P. Spokane, chose a site on the banks of a swift-flowing river. The settlement attracted many newcomers and quickly grew. Today the town they started and the river on which it's situated is named after William P. Spokane. The city of Spokane is now the second largest in Washington.

The monks retained ties to Vista House and were so fond of the beautiful area, they approached the newly established state of Washington in 1894 and conceived a system in which land could be preserved for use by the public in reserves called state parks. Today, Mt. Spokane State Park is the largest state park in Washington.

For years the monks continued using Vista House as a summer retreat. Eventually they turned the property over to the state, and to this day is open for visitors to use and enjoy.

Actually…

A group of Buddhist monks living at the top of Mt. Spokane might not seem far-fetched since Tibetan Buddhist monks are known to live in cold, high-altitude villages in the Himalayas. However, Vista House was not built, nor occupied by monks. Nor was there a head monk named William P. Spokane who founded the city of Spokane.

Stonemason Einar Fieldstad was contracted to build Vista House atop 5,833 foot Mt. Spokane. He and his team completed it in 1933 using abundant stone found at the summit. It also included a fire lookout, but over time that part was removed from the structure.

It was renovated in 2002 and is managed by Mt. Spokane State Park. When snow is not a hinderance and the road to the top of Mt. Spokane is open, visitors can wander inside, as a section of Vista House is always kept open. From July 1st until Sept 15th, it can be reserved for day use activities.

Lake Coeur d'Alene

Formerly a very large bay on the coast of Washington, Lake Coeur d'Alene was formed when a landslide cut it off from the ocean. Over millions of years, plate tectonics, with an assist by post-glacial rebound caused Lake Coeur d'Alene to slowly migrate eastward.

As the Cascade Mountain Range began forming, the lake had already reached central Washington where the warm, dry climate caused it to lose 80% of its water. It became very shallow and swampy, and the water quality was much poorer than today. However, aquatic birds loved it. As it crossed the Columbia River, it picked up salmon, ancestors of today's population of landlocked kokanee salmon.

Around 15 million years ago, Lake Coeur d'Alene reached Eastern Washington and got covered with glaciers during an ice age episode. Under a thick ice layer for thousands of years, it was thought Lake Coeur d'Alene had come to an end. But when the glaciers receded, Lake Coeur d'Alene was still there and resumed its eastward migration. As the lake neared present-day Spokane, it hooked up with the Spokane River and pulled it along.

Around 4 million years ago, Lake Coeur d'Alene was halted by the steep, hilly terrain that now surrounds the lake. The tectonic pressure of the lake trying to continue its migration caused magma to rise and form volcanoes. Mt. Rathdrum, Mt. Coeur d'Alene, Mt. Spokane, Tubbs Hill and a few other peaks erupted explosively. The lake eventually settled down, ending its migration, and the volcanoes went extinct.

Thanks to its origin as a salt water bay, Lake Coeur d'Alene supplies sushi and other seafood for local restaurants. As well, a remnant population of great white sharks is responsible for several vicious attacks on swimmers every summer.

Actually…

Coeur d'Alene did not plow across the landscape from the ocean to its present location over millions of years. As well, supplying restaurants with seafood and being home to vicious, freshwater sharks are facts found only in the mind of someone who likes to tell fish tales.

However, its formation is due to an equally interesting circumstance—a geologic catastrophe known as the Lake Missoula Floods. During the most recent ice age, Glacial Lake Missoula, formed by a glacial dam, broke and flooded the Inland Northwest repeatedly. Enormous amounts of water flowed from western Montana to the Pacific Ocean, and out of this, Lake Coeur d 'Alene was formed around 12,000 to 15,000 years ago.

Because of its beauty and size, Lake Coeur d'Alene is a very popular summer destination.

The Beach at Lake Coeur d'Alene

On summer days, sunbathers and swimmers often pack the sandy beaches on Lake Coeur d'Alene's north end. This custom was originated by Native Americans well before the first White settlers entered the area. On very hot days, Coeur d'Alene tribe members, as well as their friends from the Spokane, Kootenai, Nez Perce and Kalispel tribes crowded onto the beach to swim, tan and play beach volleyball.

As Whites entered the area and settled, they saw how fun it looked, so they, too, adopted the Native tradition of going to the beach on a hot day. However, it wasn't long before Native Americans, unaccustomed to the practice of laying towels in the sand to mark territory, found themselves excluded from the best spots.

By the late 19th century, whole sections of beach were often cordoned off for company picnics, family reunions and get-togethers of families with lots of children. Native Americans were bumped to the fringes where the beach was steep and rocky. Eventually, Natives were elbowed off the fringe areas as well.

With beach privileges lost, the Coeur d'Alene Tribe retreated to the south end of the lake and pondered how to spend hot, summer days. Tribal elders decided to build a lodge in a cool and shady spot for a time-honored, traditional activity—gambling.

It took awhile, but eventually the White population started coming for a piece of the action, and the tribe could see the same thing happening again. This time they took advantage. Forming a corporation with tribal management, the Coeur d'Alenes built a much larger, modern building, allowing their White neighbors in, but operating and profiting from the enterprise.

Getting together with all their friends from neighboring tribes for a day at the beach is nothing but a distant memory, but it has led to a new pastime—managing all the earnings the casino is bringing in.

Actually…

The lake was an important resource for the Coeur d'Alene Tribe (Schitsu'umsh in Native language). Many tribal members lived on the lake's shore. At certain times of the year, neighboring tribes traveled to the lake and gathered with the Schitsu'umsh for contests and other activities. However, there's no evidence they played volleyball.

The tradition among Whites of going to the beach specifically for recreation took root in Great Britain in the late 18th century when the belief arose that it was good for your health. The sandy, public beach at Lake Coeur d'Alene, which extends from The Coeur d'Alene Resort to the Spokane River outlet has been used for decades and is considered one of the best beaches in the Inland Northwest. It is a very popular spot on warm, summer days.

Coeur d'Alene Carousel

Hand carved and completed in 1486, the Coeur d'Alene Carousel is the first carousel ever made. Inspired by frolicking, playful horses in a farmyard pen, Italian artist Enrico Spaghetti's creation was installed in Naples to honor the animals' beauty and strength.

Mimicking the motion of horses running and jumping, the carousel was designed to be watched, not ridden. However, mischievous Naples teenagers jumped over a barrier and hopped on, breaking the fragile carvings. Realizing the potential to make good money, Enrico Spaghetti had the carousel removed to make the carvings ridable. Unfortunately, a petting zoo took its place and its popularity prevented the carousel from returning. Other artists took advantage of his idea and made lots of money building carousels, Meanwhile, Enrico Spaghetti's sat inside a barn on his property for over four centuries.

Spaghetti's descendants were cleaning out the barn one weekend when they came across the carousel, not realizing it was the first one ever built. Wanting only to be rid of it, they placed an ad in a carnival industry publication. An alert employee at Playland Pier in Coeur d'Alene put in an offer that brought the carousel to the amusement park located on a pier on Lake Coeur d'Alene. After some maintenance work, the carousel was put into service in 1942.

By 1974, termites had weakened the pier decking to such an extent that one evening the carousel broke through with a crash heard throughout downtown. It sank to the bottom of the lake, and the deep, murky water made raising the carousel impossible. With its top attraction missing, Playland Pier was forced out of business.

Thought gone for good, the carousel was actually in a state of arrested decay as it sat at the frigid lake bottom. On the afternoon of June 2nd, 2017, when the temperature hit a record high of 105 degrees, it suddenly popped to the surface looking little changed from the day it sank out of sight.

Dozens of eager enthusiasts jumped into the water, corralled the carousel and steered it to the beach. From there, they carried it a few feet at a time across the sand, over the retaining wall and left it overnight in the park. The next day they returned and carried it bit by bit to a spot near Memorial Field. In just a week's time, the carousel was cleaned up, a structure built and on June 9th, 2017, it was offering rides again.

Actually…

The Coeur d'Alene Carousel isn't really the world's first carousel, nor was it made by an Italian artist with the last name of Spaghetti. It's a 20-horse, 2-chariot, carved, merry-go-round built in New York in 1922. Designed for use at traveling carnivals, it was already part of a downtown Coeur d'Alene amusement park when it was moved in 1942 onto a pier that was built at Independence Point. That amusement park was named Playland Pier and ceased operation in the mid-1970s, after which the carousel was removed. A short time later, in 1975, the pier on which the amusement park sat was destroyed by fire.

In 1986 the carousel reappeared — for sale in Puyallup, Washington. It was purchased by a couple from Oregon who collect carousels to lease out around the country.

In 2010, a pair of carousel fans in Coeur d'Alene discovered its existence and started a campaign to bring it back. A local couple heard of the campaign and bought the carousel. They immediately donated it to the newly formed Carousel Foundation. The carousel sat in storage a few years until a permanent site, funding and constructing a facility could be completed. On June 9, 2017, the grand opening at Memorial Plaza attracted over 1,700 who rode for free.

Coeur d'Alene Resort

It was Duane Hagadone's dream to build a hotel that right off the bat would be considered the world's finest resort hotel. With completion of the 18-story tower in 1986, becoming No. 1 seemed assured. However, injuries to key housekeeping associates and a work stoppage by paper towel dispenser refill personnel hampered the resort.

During a convention for graffiti artists, a bartender slighted a group for leaving no tip. Late at night the group expressed their displeasure with spray paint. The result was a partial shutdown and days and days of wall-scrubbing inside and out. When the Top 25 World's Finest Resort Hotel final rankings came out, The Coeur d'Alene Resort had sunk to No. 21. Fans were disappointed and upset. Critics mocked the poor performance. A meme of the hotel comparing it to a rundown, boarded-up house went viral. Hagadone considered resigning.

In the off-season, resort staff trained intensively. They worked to memorize guest names permanently after one encounter. A cleaning routine was perfected that left rooms more sterile than an aseptic research laboratory. The valet team got colorful new uniforms. In its second year, the Coeur d'Alene Resort was No. 18 in the World's Finest Resort Hotel preseason rankings. They moved up steadily and by mid-season reached the No. 9 spot. As the crucial end of season Labor Day weekend approached, an August slump caused the resort to slip to No. 14.

Duane Hagadone held a team meeting and delivered an inspirational speech. Associates hustled like never before. Many had season bests. The final poll ranked the resort at No. 7. With a great final ranking, heavily recruited new talent chose to work at The Coeur d'Alene. Many top associates chose to return for the next season.

The talented team was rewarded with a No. 3 preseason ranking which caused a big sales increase and a leap in convention business. Halfway through the season, the resort moved into the No. 1 spot for the first time. The Coeur d'Alene easily qualified for post-season competition, and went on a streak, defeating bigger, more famous resorts. They reached the pinnacle Concierge Bowl, competing against defending champion and overwhelming favorite, Hotel Super Grand Diamond of The Bahamas.

On Concierge Bowl weekend, guests flocked to the Coeur d'Alene Resort. The average tip rose 17%. Negative remarks on guest surveys dived to a season low. Food and beverage went the entire weekend with no spills. With a record TV audience watching, The Concierge Bowl ended with the deciding announcement: The Coeur d'Alene Resort was international champion. No resort had ever done so in only its third year of existence.

The Coeur d'Alene Resort now has many international championships under its belt and with such a winning tradition, the resort has entered an even more competitive division—World's Finest Apartment Building. Starting next year, an international championship is the goal with the opening of The Coeur d'Alene Apartment Complex.

Actually…

The Coeur d'Alene Resort is the brainchild of Coeur d'Alene native Duane Hagadone who died in 2021 at age 87. One of his goals was for his resort to be recognized as the best in the world. However, he couldn't judge his progress using the weekly Top 25 rankings of the World's Finest Resort Hotels. Such a poll doesn't exist, nor does an end of season competition called The Concierge Bowl.

Hagadone acquired the 7-story North Shore Resort that formerly occupied the spot in 1983. He remodeled it and then built and opened the 18-story tower in 1986. The Coeur d'Alene Resort has become a world renowned hotel, and when Condé Nast Traveler named it both America's top mainland resort and the world's top travel product, Hagadone had accomplished his goal.

Coeur d'Alene Floating Green

The "floating" green at the Coeur d'Alene Resort Golf Course is actually a small island created about 4 million years ago when a cinder cone formed just offshore.

The cinder cone eventually went dormant, and when the golf course was under construction, the cone was leveled and the cinders sold as souvenirs at the course gift shop.

A few years after it was manicured into a beautiful golfing green, the cone came to life, and small eruptions began occurring regularly. Even though the vent is filled in and covered with grass, during volcanic activity it opens up and is often mistaken for the hole. Golfers trying to retrieve their golf balls have been treated for burns. When the vent is spewing, golfers have been struck by lava, requiring first aid.

Oddly, during eruptive phases, course use rises. Because of the additional hazards, par for the hole is increased from 3 to 5. Beside the scenic wonder of playing in the middle of an eruption, golfers relish the challenge of getting a good score while avoiding bursts of flying lava and superheated gases.

Actually...

The 14th hole is a floating green, not an island. And people, not volcanic activity created the green. It was put into place in 1991. A floating green was resort owner Duane Hagadone's idea and is the only one in the world. It has succeeded in making the Coeur d'Alene Resort Golf Course well known and a destination for golfers from afar.

Fort Sherman

General William Sherman, a Union commander during the Civil War, passed by Lake Coeur d'Alene in 1877 and was so impressed by the natural beauty that he ordered the construction of a resort for military officers. The following year Camp Coeur d'Alene was built. Its sole purpose was to serve as a summer holiday resort for military brass and higher-ups. In 1879, General Sherman instructed Camp Coeur d'Alene to be renamed Fort Coeur d'Alene so the public would perceive it was less like a summer camp and more like a military base.

Over the next couple decades, thousands of high-ranking officers and military leaders stayed at Fort Coeur d'Alene. The daily routine included a morning dip in the lake followed by a nature walk, and then a fishing contest. After lunch and a thirty-minute nap period, participants could choose from a float down the Spokane River, a cavalry versus infantry soccer game or crocheting classes.

Many attendees considered their visit to Fort Coeur d'Alene the highlight of the year. When General Sherman retired from military service in 1887, the army honored his brilliant camp idea by renaming the resort Fort Sherman.

By the turn of the century, warm weather locales had become a more desired vacation experience and Fort Sherman was shuttered. In its place, the army opened a new spot in southern Florida, Fort Sunny Beaches.

Actually…

General William Sherman traveled to Lake Coeur d'Alene in 1877 and issued orders for a fort to be constructed. It was called Camp Coeur d'Alene when it was completed in 1878, though the name was changed to Fort Coeur d'Alene the following year.

General Sherman retired in 1884. In 1887, the fort's name was changed again to honor his career accomplishments, not because he started a fun-filled resort for Army higher-ups. Native Americans, however, surely disagree about giving any honor to General Sherman, who worked aggressively to subdue tribes and force them onto reservations while giving little respect to previous agreements and treaties.

In its 22 years of existence, soldiers from Fort Sherman were dispatched only twice to quell potential conflicts, and both times they had little to do. The fort was decommissioned in 1900, and the property sold at auction in 1905. Today the site is occupied by North Idaho College. Visitors can still see 3 of the fort's original buildings that remain on and near campus grounds.

Fort Sherman Chapel

A minister passing through what is now Coeur d'Alene was asked by soldiers to stay and minister to them at the newly established Fort Sherman. He agreed and in 1880, Fort Sherman Chapel was quickly built. It was a magnet from day one. Soldiers flocked despite an entrance fee of fifteen cents to offset construction costs. Every service was packed. However, by 1882, soldiers were sometimes turned away. The chapel delighted the enlisted men by adding weekday services to ease overcrowding.

By 1885, pioneers were settling in the area, and the bustle at Fort Sherman Chapel increased. In response, services were offered twice a day, seven days a week. Most of the fort's soldiers eagerly attended every single service. However, some were unhappy because a tight budget caused them to miss services toward the end of the month. The chapel won their hearts by offering a volume discount plan. For $3, they could buy an unlimited monthly pass. A token for 15 services could be purchased for $1.50. The Tuesday evening service featured a drawing for a free token good for 10 services. Attendance was standing-room only every time.

The success of the Fort Sherman Chapel caught the attention of investors. A franchise agreement was drawn up, and new locations were opened. By 1897 there were a dozen Fort Sherman Chapels across the West. Competitors took notice, however, and a consortium of the Baptist, Methodist and Catholic churches bought out the chain and divvied up the locations among themselves. Thus in 1900, the Fort Sherman Chapel chain was out of business.

Actually…

The Fort Sherman Chapel was built in 1880 by the U.S. Army. However, it was never franchised, and it's unlikely soldiers were ever eager to attend services twice a day, seven days a week and pay to do so.

The chapel was abandoned when the fort closed in 1900, and it was sold at auction in 1905. It continued to be used, but slowly fell into disrepair. It was eventually purchased by The Athletic Round Table of Coeur d'Alene so that the building, which is the oldest church in the city, could be renovated. It was donated to the Museum of North Idaho in 1984 and can still be rented for events.

McEuen Park

Opened in 2014 after $20 million in improvements, McEuen is the only municipal park in the U.S. that is open to adults only. Most parks cater to children, but the city of Coeur d'Alene, in response to residents' wishes, created a park that looks like any other, but has a strict ban on children.

Coeur d'Alene residents long complained that children hog park features. They swarm over play equipment, thinking only of themselves, leaving no room for adults. Also, constantly monitoring for safety makes park visits tedious and boring. No more.

At McEuen, the giant jungle gym is sized for adults. There are swings for two, teeter-totters with cup holders and enclosed, heated slides for cold-weather use. The splash pad offers seating that is adult width. Water nozzles raised to adult height shoot powerful jets of cold water directly into the face, giving welcome relief on hot summer days.

The most popular feature is the 430-stall underground parking garage. Many adults like nothing more than driving to the park to sit in a quiet, shaded, parking spot to text and use social media. Others like napping in the designated quiet stalls. Still others enjoy hanging out, comparing their accessorized cars and shooting the breeze.

McEuen Park has been quite a success, and a fringe benefit was recently documented. While visiting the park, residents report that children are often left at home with instructions to clean house and prepare meals. Research into this arrangement found that responsibility among Coeur d'Alene children has increased 63%.

Actually…

People of all ages can go to McEuen Park. No one is posted at the park entrance refusing entry to children, so adults hoping to spend quality time together without the kids are out of luck.

There is a 430-car, below-ground garage, and perhaps a few people go there to text, use social media or sleep, but most leave the car to visit the park or places nearby.

McEuen underwent a $20 million upgrade and reopened in May of 2014 with many new features. Located downtown on the shore of Lake Coeur d'Alene adjacent to Tubbs Hill, there's no shortage of options for having a good time.

In the late 1950s, a shopping center was proposed on the land occupied by McEuen Park. However, because of the work of many, including Coeur d'Alene conservationists Art Manley and Scott Reed, the land was preserved for the future park.

Tubbs Hill

An extinct volcano, Tubbs Hill was originally named Tubbs Mountain in 1864 by a surveying party. It was much higher than now and was snow-capped most of the year.

As the city of Coeur d'Alene grew, the mountain was a convenient source of gravel for road-building and construction. Tubbs was quarried so intensely that it was completely leveled and transformed into a pit. It filled with water, and with an access road around the perimeter that kept it from merging with Lake Coeur d'Alene, its name was officially changed from Tubbs Mountain to Tubbs Lake in 1897.

Because it was warm, shallow and easily accessed, Tubbs Lake became a very popular swimming area. However, heavy use caused water quality to deteriorate, and it became very silty. Swimmers avoided the unappealing waters and eventually the lake became swampy. In 1922 the name was officially changed from Tubbs Lake to Tubbs Swamp.

It didn't take long for the swamp to naturally fill in and become a grassy meadow. It became a popular spot for kite-flyers catching breezes off Lake Coeur d'Alene, as well as a play area for dog-owners, The city council changed the name from Tubbs Swamp to Tubbs Meadow in 1938.

A post-World War II building boom brought major additions just to the east of Tubbs Meadow, which was a designated dumping spot for construction debris. In just a few years, a massive pile of tree stumps, rock and dirt accumulated until the site could hold no more. By 1953, the unsightly pile was considered a blight on an otherwise lovely lakeside town. A reclamation project was undertaken in which the pile was contoured and planted with native trees and vegetation.

A hiking path was constructed around the perimeter, and as the site slowly morphed from a debris pile to an attractive natural area, the city renamed Tubbs Meadow to its present-day name—Tubbs Hill.

Actually…

Tubbs Hill is not an extinct volcano, a former mountain, lake, swamp or meadow. It has always been a hill and these days, a protected 120-acre natural area occupies most of it. The rocky, forested area has a 2.2-mile main trail around the perimeter and several miles of secondary trails which crisscross the hill.

It was purchased and platted in 1884 by Tony Tubbs, an early Coeur d'Alene resident who planned to sell the lots to out-of-town buyers without informing them it was rocky, hilly and virtually unbuildable. Tubbs sold a few lots, but his scheme to unload the entire development and make a killing didn't work out. Thanks to his failure, the hill stayed mostly undeveloped until it was eventually purchased by the city and designated a natural area that is popular with Coeur d'Alene residents and out-of-town visitors alike.

Mineral Ridge

Formerly located near Kellogg, Idaho, Mineral Ridge was dismantled, transported and reassembled at its current site on Lake Coeur d'Alene.

Thought to have a rich deposit of minerals (thus the name), its failure to produce disgusted Kellogg-area miners. Wanting no more than to be rid of it, a deal was made in which it was shipped away, allowing the ground beneath to be prospected.

Meanwhile, Lake Coeur d'Alene gained a very attractive ridge that gave excellent views. Local leaders envisioned construction of a knock-out hiking trail that would bring visitors to the area.

Eventually funding was found, and the Mineral Ridge Trail has become very popular. On weekends, the large parking lot often fills to capacity. The hilly, 3.3 mile trail is a workout, yet doable for hiking newbies. The only downside is when old-timers take to the trail who remember the ridge when it was in Kellogg, and it faced the opposite direction. Search and rescue is often called when the confused and disoriented old timers become lost.

Actually…

Mineral Ridge was formed at its present location, and the route is so simple that search and rescue never has to be called, even when confused old timers are hiking.

The hiking area was the first developed recreation site on BLM land in Idaho when it was constructed in 1963. In 1982, the trail was named a National Recreation Trail. The 3.3-mile loop trail takes you to the top of the ridge with an elevation gain of several hundred feet.

A short drive from Coeur d'Alene, the trail is well used year-round. There are bathrooms, a picnic area and paved parking at the trailhead. The great view from the top and large, old-growth trees make it an enjoyable hike.

End Notes

In the mid-'90s, I read a booklet from the library about the history of Spokane through its landmarks. I got the idea to spoof this form of history-telling as the brief landmark descriptions would be a good way to express my sense of humor. In a short time I wrote several on yellow notebook paper, and for more than 2 decades they sat inside a cardboard storage box.

Other projects took the attention of my part-time writing career. One of them, *50 Hikes for Eastern Washington's Highest Mountains,* a hiking guide published in 2003 and now out of print, took a lot of time. I had to hike to the top of every one of the highest 50 mountains in Eastern Washington, not to mention all the driving I had to do and the rest I needed afterward. What a time gobble-upper that was.

Born, raised and a resident of the Inland Northwest for all but 7 years of my life, I'm a fan of our region and its history. With a lot of experience parodying myself for laughs, parodying my hometown was an appealing project, if I could just get around to it.

When I joined a work conference call one morning about scheduling, I suddenly had time to end my 2-decade delay. The real purpose of the call was to tell everyone their jobs were being eliminated.

From that cardboard storage box I pulled the handwritten descriptions I'd jotted down so long ago. I had a lot more to do, and I needed to read the real histories to give me ideas on how best to spoof them.

Originally, the entire book was going to be nothing but a satire of local history. However, the more I read, the more interesting the real histories were to me. I came across new stuff I that I didn't know. I decided including the real histories would be a great addition.

Several landmarks have come into existence during my lifetime and merely consulting my memory brought forth some facts. I was a high school student during Expo '74, which spawned Riverfront Park and a few of its landmarks.

However, I did very little original research. I relied on the work of mostly local writers of regional history whose work, for the most part, is easily accessible online. Hoorah to all of 'em for making my job so much easier!

Now that the book has come to fruition and its purpose, the same as many of my other writing endeavors — to make people laugh; I imagine a few may take offense. If you have an affinity for one or more of the landmarks and making fun of it rubs you the wrong way, please accept my apology. It's not done because of a lack of appreciation.

The beautiful setting, the people who worked to create these landmarks, as well as others not mentioned in this book leaves me appreciative that some people are doers, not just observers such as myself. To those who've made our cities a great place to live, I say thank-you.

Jim Johnson

Jim Johnson graduated from John Rogers High School and earned degrees from Washington State University in Pullman and Eastern Washington University. After *50 Hikes for Eastern Washington's Highest Mountains*, this is his second book. He has two adult children, really enjoys hiking, makes himself go running, which he's been doing since high school, and grows lots of stuff in his backyard vegetable garden. He's not a morning person, so consumption of coffee and perusing the Spokesman-Review are the top accomplishments on a typical morning. Since 2013 he has written a blog in the same vein as this book, imustruneverywhere.com, which consists of mostly absurd, satirical posts about running.